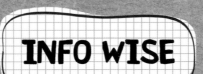

INFO WISE

IDENTIFY AND EVALUATE ADVERTISING

~Valerie Bodden~

Lerner Publications ◆ Minneapolis

For Josh and our little projects—Hannah, Elijah, Titus, and Chloe

Lerner Publications Company
A division of Lerner Publishing Group, Inc.
241 First Avenue North
Minneapolis, MN 55401 USA

For reading levels and more information, look up this title at www.lernerbooks.com.

Main body text set in Adrianna Regular 11/18. Typeface provided by Chank.

Library of Congress Cataloging-in-Publication Data

Bodden, Valerie.
    Identify and evaluate advertising / by Valerie Bodden.
        pages   cm. — (Info wise)
    Includes index.
    ISBN 978-1-4677-5226-8 (lib. bdg. : alk. paper)
    ISBN 978-1-4677-6230-4 (eBook)
    1. Advertising—Juvenile literature. I. Title.
    HF5829.B63 2015
    659.1—dc23   2014016135

Manufactured in the United States of America
1 — CG —12/31/14

CONTENTS

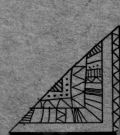

INTRODUCTION

ADVERTISING EVERYWHERE

Quick: name an ad, any ad.

That was probably pretty easy, huh?

If you've turned on the TV, listened to the radio, watched a movie, surfed the Internet, played a video game, opened a newspaper, read a magazine, walked down the street, gone into a store, or even looked at someone's T-shirt today, then you've probably already seen an ad. In fact, you've probably seen hundreds—maybe even thousands—of them since you woke up. According to media experts, we all see anywhere from three thousand to five thousand ads every day. That adds up to more than a million ads a year!

Ads are so common that we probably don't even notice many of them. And even if we do notice them, we may not realize they are ads. You probably don't think of yourself as an ad. But look down at your clothes. Are you wearing a logo or a company name? If so, then you are a walking advertisement.

But so what? Does it really matter if we are surrounded by ads? Does it make a difference if we know that what we are reading, seeing, or hearing is an advertisement? As a matter of fact, it does. Ads are intended to persuade you to think something, to do something, or to buy something. If you don't recognize a message as advertising, you may be persuaded to do what it says without considering whether doing so will be in your best interest. But if you can recognize and understand advertising messages, you'll be better equipped to decide for yourself whether to be influenced by them.

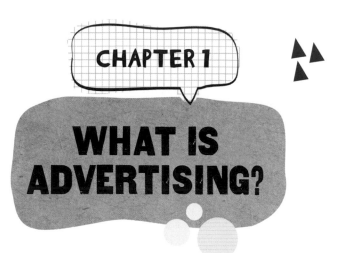

CHAPTER 1

WHAT IS ADVERTISING?

Every year, companies pour more than $500 billion into producing and distributing ads around the world. Why? It's simple: they want to convince you to buy their products. You may not just stumble across those products on your own. And even if you do stumble across them, you may not think you need them. And you may not choose to buy one company's product instead of a competitor's. Ads are meant to move the odds in a company's favor, so that you will look for that company's product, think you need it, and choose it over another company's similar product.

Ads often provide information about a product. But at their heart, ads are a form of persuasive communication. Their goal is to influence you.

Advertising can also be designed to make you loyal to a specific brand or company. When companies advertise a brand, they may focus more on their company logo or slogan than on the specific product they are selling. The idea is to form a relationship with you. The company wants to make you loyal to its brand, so that you would never even think of buying a different one. Take a second to think about the brands of shoes or clothing you buy. What makes you choose those brands over others?

ADS PAY FOR CONTENT

Although you might be annoyed whenever a commercial interrupts your favorite TV show, that commercial helps pay for the costs of producing and airing the show. Advertisers pay television stations or online video companies to air their ads at certain times of the day or during specific TV shows. In return, the advertisers are provided with a built-in audience. Newspapers, magazines, and many websites work in the same way. Without ads, access to some media content might be more expensive for consumers.

COST OF A THIRTY-SECOND TV AD IN 2013

Program	Cost
Prime-time sitcom	$62,370 to $326,260
NBC Sunday Night Football	$570,000 (average)

Sources: "Official 2013-2014 Primetime Fall Schedule," *Adweek*, October 13, 2013, http://www.adweek.com/files/upfront-sked-2013.jpg; Anthony Crupi, "The Big Bang Theory Gets the Highest Ad Rates outside the NFL: A Pricing Guide to the 2013–2014 Broadcast Season," *Adweek*, October 13, 2013, http://www.adweek.com/news/television /big-bang-theory-gets-highest-ad-rates-outside-nfl-153087.

Advertising also helps keep the economy going. Advertising is a big industry that provides jobs for many people. Ads also convince people to buy products and services. If people didn't buy those products and services, companies might go out of business.

Finally, advertising contributes to popular culture. Many advertising campaigns produce sounds and images that reflect the world around them. And major ad campaigns might be seen by people around the world, helping to connect them through shared experiences. Some people even consider advertising an art form in itself. Every year, the CLIO Awards honor the most original and creative ads in a number of mediums.

AIMING AT THE TARGET MARKET

Advertisers are interested in reaching the people most likely to buy their products. These people are known as the target market. How do companies define their target market? They do research. They might conduct surveys or polls. They try to figure out who buys products similar to theirs—or who they might convince to start buying them. A company that makes ice skates might target young figure skaters or hockey players, for instance.

Once advertisers have figured out who belongs to the target market for a specific product, they have to come up with an ad that will appeal to those people. So they do more research. They learn what the people in their target market like and don't like. They figure out what kinds of techniques are likely to persuade them.

Advertisers also consider their target market when they choose where to place their ads. They want to put their ads in the media sources most used by their target market. There wouldn't be much point in advertising denture cream in your favorite magazine, for example. You're just not likely to buy that product.

IN THE BULL'S-EYE

Guess which group is the biggest target market out there? Did you guess your own age group? If so, you're right! It turns out that young people collectively have control over a whole lot of money. In 2013, according to the Media Education Foundation, young people between the ages of eight and twelve (referred to as tweens by advertisers) spent about $43 billion of their own money. Teens spend another $155 billion a year.

Advertisers know that you sometimes beg your parents to buy you things. Advertisers even have a name for this habit. They call it pester power or the nag factor. Tweens and teens together are thought to influence about $200 billion in spending each year through the power of pestering.

Advertisers are also well aware that kids have less experience with advertising than adults and therefore may be more easily influenced by it. In fact, studies have shown that before the age of about eight, most kids believe that ads simply present factual information. They do not recognize that the ads are trying to persuade them to buy something. And even after that age, young people may not take time to think critically about the ads they are seeing.

EVALUATING ADS

So you know that advertisers are out there. You know they're researching you and trying to figure out how to make you want to buy their products. What can you do about it?

Well, the first step is to train yourself to recognize advertising when you see it. Once you have identified an ad, evaluate it. Ask yourself questions about the ad.

- *Who is responsible for the ad?* You can often identify an ad's origin by looking for a logo or a company name. Once you know who made the ad, remind yourself that the ad reflects the company's viewpoint. If the ad is for a certain brand of jeans, of course it will say that those jeans are the best.

- *What kinds of techniques does the ad use to get my attention?* Does the ad have special visual effects? Does it have a great sound track or a catchy jingle? Knowing *how* an ad is trying to persuade you can help you understand your reaction to it.

- *What is the ad really saying?* Along with noticing how an ad attracts your attention, think about what the ad is saying. Does the ad promise that if you buy a certain product you'll feel happy? Or maybe it suggests that you won't be cool unless you use this product. Think about this claim. Is it logical? Do you believe it?

- *What does the ad leave out?* Does the ad tell you everything there is to know about the product? What might the advertiser have failed to mention? Could there be negative aspects of the product that the advertiser doesn't want you to know?

This ad invites you to enter a video contest. That request is the advertisement's call to action.

- *What does the advertiser want you to do?* If the goal of every ad is to get you to do something, then you need to figure out what that something is. This is known as the call to action. Is the ad telling you to "buy one today" or to "click for more information"? When you know what an advertiser wants you to do, you can make an informed decision about whether to do it.

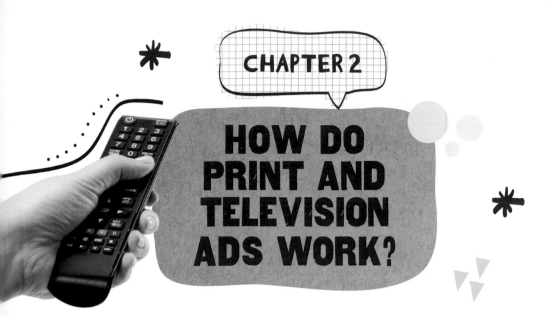

CHAPTER 2

HOW DO PRINT AND TELEVISION ADS WORK?

Have you ever noticed that if you see an ad for a product in one place, you'll probably see ads for that same product in other places too? Maybe you see a TV commercial for your favorite soft drink. When you check the weather online, you see an ad for the same soft drink. Then, on the way to school, you hear a radio ad for it too. When you get to school, there's a poster with the soft drink logo on it. Advertisers don't want you to forget about their product. So they try to keep it in front of you as often as possible and in as many different places as possible. Advertisers use the term *placement* to refer to the process of distributing ads. All of an ad's placements combined make up an ad campaign.

Even packaging can serve as advertising. If you see someone carrying a branded bag of fast food, you're reminded of that fast-food chain. Maybe seeing it even makes you crave french fries. And perhaps you convince your family to have dinner at that chain. That's exactly what the advertisers hope to achieve.

I SAW IT ON TV

You've probably seen enough TV commercials to know how television advertising works. Companies typically purchase thirty-second spots to air ads during breaks in TV shows. These commercials are usually pretty easy to spot. The show stops while the commercials are aired, and the commercials usually look or sound different from the show. You may also see commercials when you watch TV shows online. That advertising works in almost the same way. With online TV ads, you can click on the ad to learn more about the product. Sometimes you can even choose which commercial to view!

So can you pick out a TV commercial? Great! You're halfway there! Next time, don't just watch it. Think about it too. Say you see a candy bar ad. Who created the ad? *The candy bar manufacturer.* What do they want you to think about their product? *That it's the most delicious candy bar ever.* What is the ad really saying? *Your hunger won't be satisfied until you eat this candy bar.* What information might the ad have left out? *A candy bar isn't the most nutritious choice to satisfy your hunger.* What does the advertiser want you to do? *Buy a candy bar.*

Informational television, such as news programs or documentaries, sell ad time too. In fact, you may be led to believe that a show's producers endorse, or approve of, the product being advertised. After all, why would the producers allow a company to advertise during their show if they didn't like the products being advertised? The answer is easy: money.

Making documentaries can be expensive. And they don't often make a lot of money. In recent years, some documentary makers have accepted corporate sponsorships to fund projects. This means that in return for funding, the corporations can associate themselves with the documentary. Such associations can enhance a company's public image. But they can also give the impression that the documentary makers approve of the corporate sponsor.

Say a corporation sponsors a documentary about cancer. You would probably assume that the filmmakers approve of this company as one that works to fight cancer. You might even assume that the company sponsored the film because they want to support the cause of fighting cancer. But what if you learned that the company sells products that have been shown to increase the risk of developing cancer?

Whenever you see a corporate sponsor listed for an informational show, do some digging. Look up the corporation online. Its website will probably promote its positive aspects, so check some other sources, such as newspaper articles, as well. Can you find any evidence that this sponsor really supports the cause being documented, or is the company simply looking to improve its image?

INFOMERCIALS AND PRODUCT PLACEMENTS

Have you ever seen an infomercial? That's one of those half-hour-long commercials that touts a specific product, such as a home gym or a set of knives. An infomercial is often set up like a talk show or an interview. Or it might seem like an educational show. The speakers usually present a lot of factual information. But there is a call to action too: "Order yours now!" When you hear that call to action, stop and think. What is the ad telling you to do? Why is the ad saying you should do this? What kind of benefit does the infomercial say you will

Host Tracy Metro (left) interviews actor Mr. T (right) in this infomercial for the FlavorWave Turbo Oven.

get? Is it likely that the product will really deliver that benefit?

While commercials and infomercials can be fairly easy to spot, product placement is trickier. Have you ever been watching a TV show and noticed that your favorite character was eating a Subway sandwich or driving a Ford? Or maybe he pulled out an iPad or wore Nikes. These are all examples of product placement. Companies often pay for such placements. Or a company provides free items for the show to use.

Why would companies do this? The idea is that you will see these products in a show you love and associate them with the good feelings you have for the show. You might even think that owning these items will make you more like the characters in the show. And you can't fast-forward through product placements as you can with commercials. If you aren't actively analyzing product placements as ads, you might be more easily swayed by them.

But now that you've started watching for product placements, you can evaluate them. Whenever you see a specific branded product pop up, ask yourself what it's doing there. Consider whether a company may have provided it—and why.

Product placements can be found on some news shows too. The anchors on a local morning news program might have a cup of coffee from McDonald's in front of them. Or a news show might do a segment on several local businesses. It may or may not disclose that the businesses have paid to be featured. Whenever you see a product or a company on a news show, try to evaluate the content. Is it objective? Or does it reflect the company's point of view? Is the footage meant to motivate you to buy something?

In both newspapers and magazines, some ads are even laid out to look like articles. Such ads are known as advertorials (the print equivalent to infomercials). Sometimes they have the word *advertisement* in small print—but it might be hard to spot. As with other ads, ask yourself who wrote the content, what the ad is really saying, and what it's trying to get you to do.

A magazine advertisement that looks like an article is called an advertorial.

ADVERTISING AND MEDIA BIAS

So you've learned to pick out ads on TV and in print. But there's one more thing you should be aware of. Sometimes, advertisers can have a powerful impact on the editorial content of a show or an article. Since advertisers invest thousands of dollars in their ads, the advertisers want to make sure they appear in the most favorable context possible. Fast-food advertisers, for instance, wouldn't want their ads to appear next to an article discussing health problems that can come from eating fast food. Advertisers might not even want it to appear in the same paper! So they might pressure the newspaper to change or cut the story. In extreme cases, advertisers might threaten to withdraw their ads if the newspaper or news program doesn't change its content. Such advertiser influence can lead to media bias.

The danger is that even if consumers know not to take what an ad says at face value, people generally trust what newspapers, magazines, and news programs tell them. When a magazine reviews a product, such as a video game, we believe that its review is objective and unbiased. But what if the video game manufacturer is one of the magazine's major advertisers? Does that impact the magazine's review of the product? It might. Or it might influence which video games get reviewed at all.

How can you tell if a media report has been influenced by advertising? It can be tough, but you can look for ads by the manufacturer in the magazine. You can also compare the magazine's review to other reviews. Different media sources and other consumers—your friends or even strangers—may have

posted reviews online. And if you decide to buy the game, you can compare your experience with the magazine's review.

Although magazines and newspapers account for most print advertising, you can also find print ads on billboards, posters, leaflets, store displays, and more. So pay close attention to what you read. Just because it's in print doesn't mean it's true. And it doesn't mean you have to buy anything!

AN ARTICLE OR AN AD?

Some print ads are easy to recognize. They may be in a separate box in a newspaper, or they may display a prominent logo or call to action. But other ads are more subtle. In magazines, especially, the photos in an ad can look much like the photos in the rest of the magazine.

Take a look at the pages to the right. They are from a teen fashion magazine. The page on the left offers makeup application tips. Although it does list product brand names, it is still considered part of the magazine's content, not an ad. The page on the right is trickier, though. The picture at the top looks very much like the photos on the left page. The makeup shown on the page looks like the makeup on the left page. So is the right-hand page part of the magazine's content, or is it an ad?

Let's figure it out. Do you see a logo or a company name? Yes. The brands CoverGirl and Herbal Essences are both listed prominently. Another clue is how the products are displayed. On the left page, the product names

are listed in very small, plain black type. The right page shows pictures of the products themselves, with bright colors and descriptive text. Finally, if you're still not sure, look around for an advertising label. In this ad, note the word *advertisement* in the upper right corner of the page.

Ads also want to convince you to do something. In this ad, the text is yet another push to use these products. See the bold type on this page? It's reminding you, yet again, that you should buy and use these products if you want to look gorgeous.

CHAPTER 3

WHERE ARE ADS ONLINE?

The Internet is the fastest-growing advertising medium, with ads springing up in banners, on company websites, in text, in games, and on social media sites. Unlike television and print, the Internet is interactive. It allows consumers to interact with content through games, surveys, registration forms, and more. And it allows companies to collect information about the people who are interacting with their ads—information that can help them create and distribute even more ads.

SPONSORED RESULTS, BANNER ADS, AND POP-UPS

Say you're doing a research report and you go online to find some information. The first place you'll probably check is a search engine. That's a good idea. But before you start clicking on the links that come up, you should know that the first few are usually sponsored results. That means those sites have paid to be listed first in the search results, often because they hope to sell you something. Say that you are looking for information on training a dog. The first several results in most search engines will probably be links to dog training programs or even to pet stores. Fortunately, sponsored results generally appear in a separate box or have the words *sponsored* or *ad* in small print to help you identify them as advertisements. So be sure to look carefully before you click on anything. Or try a kid-safe search engine that doesn't feature sponsored results, such as Google Junior or KidRex.

Banner ads are so common and so easy to spot as ads that Internet users often ignore them. These are the ads that appear in a separate box, or banner, at the top or side of a website. The box may or may not be identified with the word *advertisement.* But you will probably see a company or product name or logo. The advertiser's goal is to get you to click on the ad, which will take you to a page with more information about the product.

Can you spot the banner ads on this site? What are they trying to sell you? Why do you think the advertiser chose to advertise on this site?

Pop-up ads are similar to banner ads, except that they don't appear directly on a web page. Instead, they pop up in a small box in front of the content you're viewing. This makes them harder to ignore than banner ads. But many software programs offer pop-up blockers to stop these ads from ever appearing on your screen.

NATIVE ADS

Unlike banner ads and pop-ups, which are set apart from the rest of a website, native ads can be tricky to identify. They are usually woven right into a site's content. They might appear as recommended links in the middle of an article you are reading. These ads might be text, images, or videos. They may or may not be set off by a box. They may or may not be identified with the word *advertisement.*

A particularly tricky form of native advertising is in-text ads. With an in-text ad, words in the text of an article are hyperlinked. You might expect to click on the hyperlinked word to get more information about the topic. But when you mouse over or click on some hyperlinked words, you will see an ad instead.

How can you tell if you're looking at legitimate additional information about a topic or at an ad? For starters, was the word in the text underlined twice? That can be a clue that it leads to an ad. Also, pay attention to what comes up. Does it have anything to do with the word you clicked on? Is it in the right context? For example, if the article is about Windows, the computer operating system, and you get a link to a window manufacturer, you're probably looking at an ad. Or say you clicked on the word *computer,* hoping to find more information about computers. But instead, you get an ad for a specific computer. How do you know it's an ad? Do you see a specific company name or logo? How about a call to action? Are you told to *do* something?

VIDEO ADS

Video ads can also be part of a site's content. Sometimes they appear in banners or along the side of a website. Other times they pop up when you click on a link within the site, and you have to watch them before you see the new page.

Video ads are often very similar in content to television commercials. But unlike TV ads, online video ads are interactive. You might be able to click on the ad for more information or to purchase something immediately. Or you can sometimes rate the ad, which provides the advertisers with real-world information on the ad's appeal and success. You can share an ad too. So many people share video ads, in fact, that many of them go viral. That means they spread around the web as quickly as a virus, as one person shares them with her friends, who share them with their friends, who share them with their friends—you get the idea. Before you know it, millions of people have seen the ad.

Before you click to rate a video ad, think about whether you want the advertiser to collect information about you. And before you tell your friends about the latest viral ad, think about what it's selling. Is it something you want to help promote?

ADVERGAMES

Do you like to play online games? They can be fun, and you can play many games for free. But do you know who sponsors that game you're playing? Advergames are online games that appear to be just for fun. But advergames also integrate a specific product or products right into the game play. Some cereal companies create whole worlds of games, with the cereal brands built in. So as you play the game, you see the cereal show up again and again. And of course you're having fun. Doesn't that make you hungry for cereal? Or a game might have ads in the background. A race car might have a logo on it, or the car might drive past a billboard advertising a product.

Some sites have other activities too, such as coloring sheets or e-cards you can send your friends. Even though these activities and games are fun, don't be fooled. They are advertising in the same

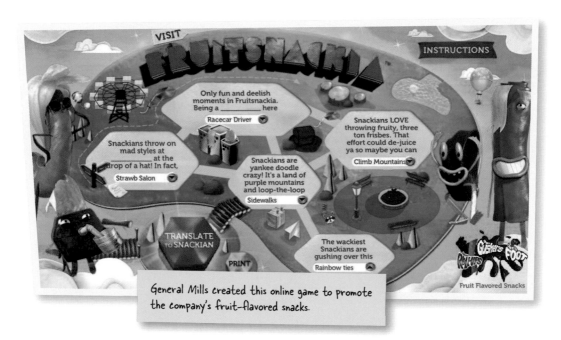

General Mills created this online game to promote the company's fruit-flavored snacks.

way a TV commercial does. So try to separate your enjoyment of the game from your desire for the product. Would you still want to buy the product if you hadn't seen it in a game?

E-MAIL AND SOCIAL MEDIA

Do you e-mail? Maybe you use YouTube or other kinds of social media. While these avenues can be handy for connecting with friends, they can also give advertisers another chance to target you. Some e-mail providers, such as Google, have programs to scan the e-mails you send and receive. The programs pick out key words that indicate your interests and habits. Knowing those key words allows advertisers to send you specifically targeted ads. So if you e-mail your friend about a song you love, you may see ads for music the next time you check your e-mail or do an online search.

Social media sites and advertisers can also monitor the websites you visit. Banner ads for products related to these sites may appear on the pages you visit. Or ads might appear in your accounts on social media sites. Your profile on social media sites also gives advertisers information that helps them choose which ads to show you.

Pay attention to the ads you see online. Do they seem to be targeted right to you? Think about how advertisers might have gotten the information they needed to direct those ads to you.

REGISTRATIONS, SWEEPSTAKES, AND COMPANY WEBSITES

Want to win a new bike? How about a year's supply of ice cream? All you have to do is fill out this form to register. It sounds easy enough. But when you fill out any kind of form online—whether it's a sweepstakes entry or a registration form for a specific site—you are providing advertisers with more information about yourself. And they can use that information to track your Internet habits and send you targeted ads. So think twice before you complete an online form or a contest entry. Do the benefits outweigh the risks of receiving even more advertising?

Sometimes you might see a print ad for a contest. These often ask you to visit a company website to submit your entry. Companies track your information with these contests too. But they have also succeeded in drawing you to their websites, where they can tell you more about their products.

LD SERIES

100s OF OTHER PRIZES

Select age ▾   ENTER NOW ▶

Official Rules | Privacy Policy | FAQ
NO PURCHASE NECESSARY. MANY WILL ENTER, FEW WILL WIN. L
years and older. Grand Prize Entry Period closes 6/30/14. Sweepstakes
inclu
Leag   LittleLeagu
                                                         ague Base

When you enter online contests, you give advertisers information they can use to send you targeted ads.

On a company's website, you probably expect to see ads. After all, the website exists to promote the company and its products. These websites might also include additional product information. But remember that this information is presented from the company's perspective. Ask yourself what information the company may have left out. Is there somewhere else you could find this information, such as in a newspaper article?

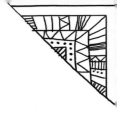

ONLINE ADS AND BIAS

As with TV and print ads, online ads can have an influence on a site's content and may lead to bias. Pay attention to how the ad's message relates to the content on the site. Is the site promoting the products highlighted in the ads? Is the advertising integrated into the site's content? Does the site seem to exclude important information that would contradict an ad? It's unlikely that an online article would provide false information to please an advertiser. But pressure from an advertiser could convince the publisher of an article to leave out details that make the advertiser's product look bad.

Say there's an ad for a soft drink right next to an online article about keeping your teeth healthy. Take a close look at the article. Does it mention that one way to keep your teeth healthy is to avoid sugary drinks? Or does it skip over that fact? It can be difficult to evaluate what is *not* on a site, but take a moment to think about the content. You can also check it against another article on the same topic. Do you find any new information that was left out of the first? Could it be because of the ads on the site?

Just because a site contains ads related to the content does not necessarily mean the site is biased, however. That's just good target marketing. So if you're on a website about cats and there happens to be a banner ad for cat toys, that doesn't necessarily indicate bias. But if you're reading an online article about the best cat toys and the top-ranked toy also happens to have an ad on the page, you might have to evaluate whether the site's content could have been influenced by the advertiser.

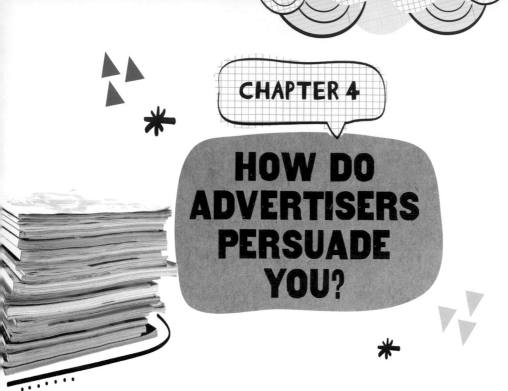

HOW DO ADVERTISERS PERSUADE YOU?

So now you know where ads are—pretty much everywhere. And you know the basics of how to recognize and evaluate them. That means you're ready to find out the specific techniques advertisers use to persuade you. Once you learn to recognize these techniques, you will be much less likely to fall for them. Then you can make informed choices about what to buy rather than purchasing something just because an ad told you to.

APPEALS TO REASON

An appeal-to-reason ad is one that tries to convince you to buy a product based on information. An ad using this technique might present facts about a product and how it works. It might list the ways the product can benefit you. By law, advertisers cannot make false claims about a product. So an advertiser cannot say that a product will make you grow several inches unless it really will make

you grow that much. But the United States has no government agency to approve ad claims before they go public, so take some time to think about what an ad is telling you. Is the claim logical? Is there any way you can double-check it?

Even though advertisers must tell the truth about products, they are allowed to use hype. That means they can make subjective claims about the items being sold, even if those claims can't be proven. So advertisers can claim that their product is the "best" or "amazing" or "beautiful." Even though these words might seem to be giving you information, they simply state an opinion—the advertisers'. The next time you spot an ad, pull out all the hype words. What's left? Does it tell you anything useful?

Sometimes advertisers try to make us think the best of their product by putting down another product. Think about political ads. Rather than focusing on themselves, politicians often point out the negatives about their competitors. Ask yourself if knowing bad things about one product or politician makes you prefer the advertised product or politician.

This negative political ad appeared on television. The ad, paid for by the candidate's rival, says that the candidate failed to vote in past local elections, which implies that he is unfit to serve in public office.

APPEALS TO EMOTION

Many ads try to connect with a consumer's emotions, such as excitement, happiness, empathy, or even fear. If an ad makes you laugh, you might remember it longer. Or an ad might appeal to your fears. If you don't use this specific toothpaste, for instance, you'll have bad breath. When you're looking at these kinds of ads, try to separate the emotional appeal from the product being advertised. Think about how you feel about the product itself rather than how the ad makes you feel.

Closely related to emotional appeals are lifestyle claims. These ads promote a certain lifestyle (fun, carefree, wealthy, or cool) and imply that a certain product can help you achieve this lifestyle. An ad might show a "perfect" family. They have a nice home, cool clothes, and great hair, and they're always happy. And what is it that helps them to be a perfect family? They have the perfect family car, of course, according to the ad. Think about what this implies. If your family buys this car, you'll have the perfect family life too. But does that claim make sense? Would owning a certain car really make your family perfect?

Advertisers especially like to play on our desire to be cool. So they'll show someone who's the opposite of cool. But when he gets that special pair of shoes, suddenly he's popular. Everyone wants to be his friend. Think about what the ad is really saying: if you get those shoes, everyone will want to be your friend too. But is that

logical? Do you choose your friends based on the shoes they wear?

Or an ad will play on the fear of being left out. Everyone else is buying this product. Why aren't you? You don't want to be the only one in your school who doesn't have this product, do you? This technique is known as "the bandwagon approach," because it's meant to make you want to jump on the bandwagon. That means you do what everyone else is doing. Again, think critically about this claim. Is it really possible that *everyone* else has bought this product? That's unlikely. And even if everyone else is doing something, is that the best reason for you to do it?

APPEAL TO CREDIBILITY

Sometimes people make decisions about what to buy based on what others say about a product. So advertisers use testimonials to persuade us.

Many testimonials feature celebrities. If your favorite athlete or movie star endorses a product, you might want to use the same product. You know that the celebrity is famous, wealthy, and a good actor or athlete. The advertiser wants you to think that if you use the same products as the celebrity, you will become famous and wealthy too. Maybe those sneakers will help you become a star tennis player!

Take a look at this ad starring NBA star Dwyane Wade. What is he promoting? Why do you think the advertiser chose Dwyane Wade to promote this product? What qualities do you associate with him? Does knowing that he likes this snack affect your feelings about it?

Celebrities also get paid to wear specific brands or to promote certain products on social media. This type of advertising is more subtle than TV commercials or print or online ads—and it can be more powerful. Since the celebrity doesn't wear a sign saying, "I was paid to use this product," you might believe that the celebrity chose it because he or she loves it. And if so, why wouldn't you? But before you go out and buy anything, consider how likely it is that the

BEYONCÉ
RISE
THE NEW FRAGRANCE

celebrity really uses this product. And if so, does that mean you should too?

Not all endorsements are by real-life celebrities. Some brands are endorsed by fictional spokescharacters. These might be characters from cartoons or movies. Or they could be spokescharacters created specifically for one brand, such as Tony the Tiger for Frosted Flakes cereal. These characters help you make a connection with the brand. But think about whether your connection is with the character or the product. Would you still like the product even if there were no spokescharacter?

SENSORY APPEAL AND REWARDS

What are some of your favorite ads? What is it that you like about them? Maybe a commercial features one of your favorite songs. Or perhaps you can't get that catchy jingle out of your head. Do you like a commercial's bright colors and fast-moving action? Can you almost taste the hamburger in the picture? Ads that appeal to our senses can be powerfully persuasive. But remember that camera and lighting tricks can make things look more appealing than they are in real life.

Advertisers might offer rewards to catch your interest too. Think of fast-food kids' meals. Do ads for these meals focus on the food or on the toys that come with it? Which is more appealing to kids?

For most ads, advertisers don't rely on just one technique. They mix and match different ideas to come up with a message designed to persuade you, the consumer.

ANALYZE YOUR ADS

With all that in mind, try to analyze the advertising techniques you see around you. Which ones do you find the most persuasive? Do you tend to fall for ads with great music? Will you buy anything promoted by your favorite star? Are you afraid of being left out? When you know which techniques affect you, you can be on the lookout for those techniques. Then remember to ask: Who made the ad? What is the ad really saying? What does it leave out? What does the advertiser want you to do?

Knowing about ads won't make them go away. In fact, you'll probably notice more ads now than ever before. But that's because you've learned what to look for and how to evaluate the ads. Feel free to question what you see on TV, what you read, and even what your friends pass on to you. Don't be afraid to disagree with ads and even to pull them apart to figure out what the advertiser really wants from you.

BRAVE
TAKES
A CHANCE.

Keds™

AVAILABLE AT NORDSTROM

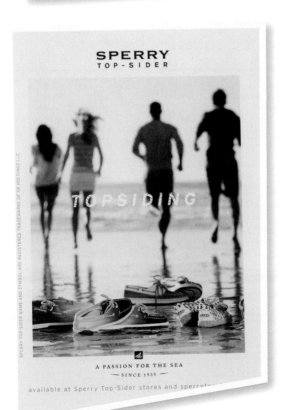

SPERRY
TOP-SIDER

TOPSIDING

A PASSION FOR THE SEA
— SINCE 1935 —

available at Sperry Top-Sider stores and sperry...

Analyzing advertisements doesn't mean you'll never buy or do anything you see advertised. But it does mean that you'll think about the ads you see before you respond to them. Maybe you'll adjust your habits to buy or do only the things that are really necessary. And that makes you a smarter consumer—of products and of information!

NOW YOU DO IT

It's your turn to identify and evaluate advertising. Find three different ads: one from TV, one in print, and one on the Internet. For each ad, identify and write down the following information:

1. Who made or paid for the ad? How can you tell?

2. What techniques does the ad use?

3. What is the ad really saying?

4. What might the ad have left out?

5. Who is the target market for the ad?

After you've evaluated each ad, decide which one you find most persuasive. Why?

GLOSSARY

bias: judging or favoring something unfairly, based on outside influence, rather than judging it based on facts

brand: a name that identifies a particular company or product

consumer: someone who uses or buys a product or a service

culture: the customs, art, skills, and ideas of a group of people from a specific time and place

distribute: to give something out

documentary: a film or a TV program about real-life events or people

economy: the system by which goods and money are produced, distributed, and consumed

endorse: to publicly recommend something, often in return for payment

hyperlink: text or images on a web page that can be clicked on to bring up another web page, document, or image

logo: a symbol used to identify a particular company or brand

media: ways of communicating information to a lot of people. The media include newspapers, television, and the Internet. Medium is the singular form of media.

objective: influenced by facts, not by emotions or bias

persuade: to convince someone to believe something or to do something

slogan: a short, easy-to-remember phrase used to advertise a specific product or brand

subjective: based on feelings or opinions

testimonial: a statement in support of something

SELECTED BIBLIOGRAPHY

Abram, Stephen. "K-12 Information Literacy: Preparing for the Dark Side." *MultiMedia & Internet@Schools* 14, no. 4 (July/August 2007): 25.

Ali, Moondore, Mark Blades, Caroline Oates, and Fran Blumberg. "Young Children's Ability to Recognize Advertisements in Web Page Designs." *British Journal of Developmental Psychology* 27, no. 1 (March 2009): 71–83.

Calvert, Sandra. "Children as Consumers: Advertising and Marketing." *Children and Electronic Media* 18, no. 1, 2008. Accessed April 12, 2014. http://www.princeton.edu /futureofchildren/publications/docs/18_01_FullJournal.pdf.

Canada's Centre for Digital and Media Literacy. "Privacy Playground Teacher's Guide." Media Smarts. 2013. Accessed April 12, 2014. http://mediasmarts.ca/sites/default/files/pdfs/games/privacy _playground_guide_%202013.pdf.

Federal Trade Commission. "Glossary." Admongo. Accessed April 12, 2014. http://www.admongo.gov/glossary.aspx.

McDonough, John, ed. *The Advertising Age Encyclopedia of Advertising.* Vol. 2. New York: Fitzroy Dearborn, 2003.

LERNER

SOURCE

Expand learning beyond the printed book. Download free, complementary educational resources for this book from our website, www.lerneresource.com.

FURTHER INFORMATION

Admongo
> http://www.admongo.gov
> Spot and analyze all the ads around you in this game created by the Federal Trade Commission.

Duke University: Ad Access
> http://library.duke.edu/digitalcollections/adaccess
> Check out all kinds of ads from the early and mid twentieth century, and consider how they're different from modern ads.

Gogerly, Liz. *Cool Brands.* Minneapolis: Lerner Publications, 2012.
> Get the inside scoop on brands and logos.

Lusted, Marcia Amidon. *Advertising to Children.* Edina, MN: Abdo Publishing, 2009. Learn more about the history of how advertisers market directly to kids and why it matters.

Media Smarts: Co-Co's AdverSmarts
> http://mediasmarts.ca/sites/default/files/games/coco/flash/start.html
> Learn more about online advertising by creating a website for a cereal brand.

PBS Kids: Don't Buy It
> http://pbskids.org/dontbuyit/advertisingtricks
> Play games and check out pictures and videos to learn more about advertising tricks and techniques.

INDEX

PHOTO ACKNOWLEDGMENTS

The images in this book are used with the permission of: © iStockphoto/Kubrak78, p. 4; © Independent Picture Service, pp. 5, 11, 16, 19, 24, 32, 33, 35; © iStockphoto/Erikona, p. 6; © iStockphoto/RuslanOmega, p. 8; © iStockphoto/pavlen, p. 12; © iStockphoto/luminis, p. 13; © David Livingston/Getty Images Entertainment/Getty Images, p. 15; © iStockphoto/LPETTET, p. 17; © iStockphoto/Liliboas, p. 20; Website © Société des Produits Nestlé S.A, p. 21; © iStockphoto/t_kimura, p. 22; © Mike Watson Images/moodboard/Thinkstock, p. 23; © iStockphoto/hocus-focus, p. 25; © Website Snyder's-Lance, Inc., p. 26; © iStockphoto/subjug, p. 28; AP Photo, p. 29; © iStockphoto/egal, p. 30; © Bennett Raglin/BET/Getty Images, p. 31; © Jon Le-Bon/Shutterstock, p. 34.

Cover and interior backgrounds: © koosen/Shutterstock (brown background); © Mrs. Opossum/Shutterstock (zig zag pattern); © AKSANA SHUM/Shutterstock (diamond pattern); © AtthameeNi/Shutterstock (blue lined graph paper); © Looper/Shutterstock (arrows); © AlexanderZam/Shutterstock (graph paper dots); © oleschwander/Shutterstock (yellow lined paper dots).